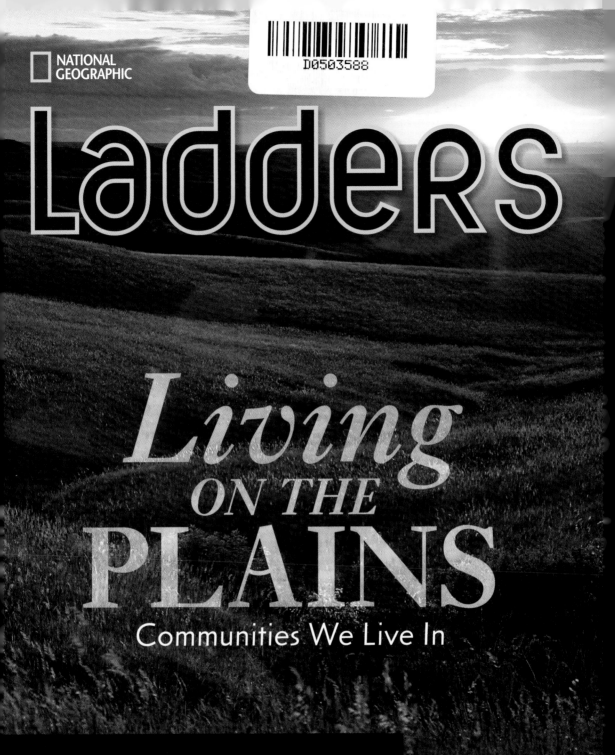

NATIONAL GEOGRAPHIC

Ladders

Living ON THE PLAINS

Communities We Live In

Prairie Dog Towns

by Debbie Nevins
illustration by Patrice Rossi Calkin

As you might guess, prairie dogs live on the **prairie**. A prairie is a type of grassland. Prairie dogs are not dogs. They are **rodents**. Rodents are small animals with big front teeth for chewing.

Black-tailed prairie dogs live in the Great Plains. This is a flat, dry, grassy part of the western United States. Prairie dogs eat grass on the Great Plains. The animals tunnel into the ground to build their homes. These homes help keep them safe.

Long ago, the Great Plains were full of prairie dogs. But people began using the land for farming and raising animals. Today there's less open land for prairie dog towns. So there are fewer prairie dogs.

< This kind of prairie dog only lives in the state of Utah. It is called a Utah prairie dog.

Home on the Range

Prairie dogs live with their families. They live in large communities called "towns." In a town, a prairie dog's underground home is a

Entrances
Burrows have at least two ways into the tunnels. These ways in are called entrances.

Listening Room
The first room in a burrow is for listening. If they hear noise outside, prairie dogs do not go out.

Nest
Babies, called pups, are born and raised in the nest.

Toilet
Prairie dogs dig a chamber to use as a toilet. They keep it clean.

burrow. It has twisty tunnels and different ways to get in. The tunnels lead to different rooms called **chambers**. Each chamber has a different use.

Dry Room Prairie dogs gather here if the burrow floods. This room is high, and it stays dry.

Bedroom The family sleeps here at night. This room is deep in the burrow.

A Prairie Dog's Day

Prairie dogs are busy in the daytime. That's when they come out to eat. They also take their pups for runs outside. To say hello, prairie dogs might touch mouths. They might even clean each other's fur.

Coyotes, foxes, and hawks hunt for prairie dogs. Prairie dogs work together to stay safe from enemies. Even with their short legs, prairie dogs can run away from enemies quickly.

This mother builds a nest. She makes it before birthing her new pups.

Prairie dogs love to eat a grass called timothy.

These friends greet each other with a "kiss."

When prairie dogs see or hear trouble, they bark warnings to others. They also bob up and down. Then the prairie dogs run into their burrows.

Prairie dogs have different warnings for different enemies. In a "jump-yip" cry, they stand on their back feet and yip loudly. The yip might tell others that a danger has passed. Being in a community is the safest life for prairie dogs.

Mothers usually check for danger outside before leaving the burrow. Then the pups come out to play if it is safe.

Check In How do prairie dogs keep themselves and their community safe?

Cyrus
HEADING

Cyrus is a 9-year-old boy. He and his family are moving from Kentucky across the Great Plains. They are headed to a new farm in Kansas. Land is cheaper there. Farms are bigger there. Their journey west is difficult but exciting.

April 24, 1870

Hooray, we're on our way! My brother, Charles, and I walk next to our wagon. We're looking for big rocks in

WEST

by Elizabeth Massie
illustrations by Craig Orback

the rough path. We don't want to break a wagon wheel.
The wagon is full of our food and furniture.

Papa rides a horse ahead of the wagon. Aunt Millie drives the
wagon. My cousins, Sissy and Pearl, ride inside.

May 16, 1870

We have traveled through Kentucky, Indiana, and Illinois.
Today, we will load our wagon onto a ferryboat. We need to
cross the Mississippi River to get to Missouri. Men use long
paddles to row the ferry across the river.

June 5, 1870

We've crossed into Kansas. Charles climbed a tree this afternoon, and he saw a big cloud. That was a windstorm coming. An hour later, it hit us.

We're inside the wagon now. The windstorm is rocking us back and forth. We look out at the storm. The sand is blowing in a little. Our mouths are covered with pillowcases to keep the sand out. Cousin Sissy says our wagon is sturdy. That makes me feel better.

We can't travel during the storm. I'm passing the time thinking and writing. Kansas looks different than Kentucky. In Kentucky, there were forests and mountains. We had neighbors on the other side of a hill. In our new state, the closest neighbor might live miles away. There are few trees in Kansas. All we see is the sky and grass of the plains.

June 21, 1870

This morning, a man told us that Arapaho
(uh-RAP-uh-hoh) Indians lived in a village
on our route. Charles and I became scared.
But Papa said, "We'll be fine. They live on the
plains, too."

Later, we saw a village of tents. People in the
village stared at us. I waved hello. I saw men
hanging large skins on sticks. Papa said they were
drying out buffalo hides. We've seen buffalo on our
trip. They have curved horns and shoulder humps.
I never saw such huge skins like those in the village.

June 26, 1870

We have reached our land! The farm has a small river. Charles and I ran to the water and dove in. It was so nice to take a bath and wash away the dust and sweat!

July 5, 1870

There aren't many trees on our land. So we built our house out of sod. Sod is grass and dirt. We cut sod bricks out of the ground. Then we stacked them to make walls. We finished yesterday.

Last night, Charles, Pearl, and Sissy fell asleep quickly. But I tossed and turned. I was excited to be sleeping inside the sod house.

When I started falling asleep, an earthworm dropped from the sod ceiling onto my face! I laughed out loud and woke everyone up.

Today, a boy named Andrew and his father visited us. Andrew lives on a farm five miles away. We played tag. He promised to lend me some books. I like it here on the Kansas plains!

Check In What new things did Cyrus see when his family reached the plains of Kansas?

Kids on the Plains

by Nathan W. James and Cynthia Clampitt

Many countries have plains. The plains of the United States are called the Great Plains. In Argentina, the plains are called the Pampas. All plains are flat and have few trees. Let's look at plains in two countries.

> The Great Plains are known for their long stretches of flat land. They also have good farming soil.

That's me

Corn, my favorite!

Hi! My name is Amanda. I live on a farm in Nebraska. Nebraska is in the American Great Plains. I see fields of green corn and golden wheat outside my bedroom window. Other corn and wheat farms surround my family's farm. Corn and wheat are used to make bread and other foods. The Great Plains are called "America's bread basket." That's because foods used to make bread are grown here.

We're having a family picnic today. Most of the food comes from the Great Plains. The beef for our hamburgers comes from our neighbor's cattle ranch. The buns are made from wheat grown nearby. The lettuce, carrots, and tomatoes come from our garden.

Wind-Blown

Fields aren't all I see outside my window. I also see **wind turbines**. These machines have blades that spin in the wind to make electricity. They look like giant metal flowers. The turbines on our land give power to our town and nearby towns. Nebraska has no mountains to block the wind. The windy plains are perfect for twirling turbines.

It looks like a flower!

The tower of a wind turbine can be as tall as a 30-story building. The blades can be as big as the wings of a large jet.

Moo!

Hola (Oh-lah)!
Hello!

My name is Mateo. I live in the "great plains" of Argentina, a country in South America. We call our plains the Pampas. They're a lot like the Great Plains in the United States. The Pampas are flat and grassy. The fields are a good place for cattle to eat grass. We also grow food here on farms.

We live on the plains. But we're just a short ride away from the mountains and the ocean. I just went hiking in the mountains with my mom. I have gone fishing in the ocean on my cousin's boat many times. It's fun!

You can walk for miles and miles on the Pampas before finding shade from a tree.

I ride horses in these hills, called "foothills." They are at the base of the Andes Mountains.

My Dad, the Gaucho

I live on an **estancia** (ay-STAN-see-ah), which is a ranch. My family raises cattle. My dad is a **gaucho** (GOW-choh), which is like a cowboy. He rides a horse to **corral** cattle. That means he brings together the cattle from all over the ranch.

Gauchos like my dad wear a wide belt to hold their tools. They tuck their pants into leather boots. When the weather is cool, gauchos wear a serape (suh-RAH-pay). That is a wool cape or coat. A gaucho uses a bola to round up cattle. Bolas are leather cords with three iron balls. My dad can throw the bola so it wraps around a cow's legs. That stops the cow from running.

serape

bolas

boots

bolas

Dad's boots

The rich, flat land of most plains is good for growing food and raising cattle. No matter where plains are located, the land shapes the lives of the people living there.

< Gauchos also use a long rope to herd cattle. They loop the end of the rope around the cow's neck. Then they guide it to safety.

Check In Compare the American Great Plains and the Pampas. How are they alike?

Discuss

1. What connections can you make among the three selections in this book? In what ways are they related?

2. How are prairie dog communities like human communities? How are they different?

3. Where did Cyrus and his family begin their journey? Where did their journey end? Compare their old farm and the land around it to their new farm and its land.

4. How does the wind play a part in life on the plains?

5. What do you still wonder about life in a plains community? How can you learn more?